TALES · FROM THE · BALLET

TALES · FROM THE · BALLET

ANTONIA BARBER

ILLUSTRATED BY
DIZ WALLIS

Kingfisher

KINGFISHER
An imprint of Larousse plc
Elsley House, 24-30 Great Titchfield Street
London W1P 7AD

First published by Kingfisher 1995
2 4 6 8 10 9 7 5 3 1

A CIP catalogue record for this book
is available from the British Library

ISBN 1 85697 361 1

Designed by Caroline Johnson
Edited by Suzanne Carnell

Printed in Italy

Contents

The Song of the Nightingale

In the ancient land of China there was once a mighty Emperor. So great was his power that no man might approach him except on bended knees, and when he rode out among his people, they bowed their heads to the ground so that his glory should not blind them. And yet, for all that, inside his gorgeous robes he was a man like any other.

He lived in a palace so splendid that word of it had spread throughout the world, and ambassadors came from other rulers to see how things were done at his court. Even the mighty Emperor of Japan sent wise men to see what they could learn from his great rival.

As these wise men drew near to the Emperor's palace, night was falling and they passed into a dark wood. In the wood lived a nightingale and the sweetness of its singing stopped them in their tracks. "How powerful this great Emperor must be," they said, "for even the birds in his forests sing more sweetly than any other birds in the world."

For many weeks the wise men stayed at the Emperor's court, marvelling at the splendour around them: at the jewelled throne and the painted dragons and the shining roofs where every tile was covered in gold. When at last the time came for them to return home, the Emperor asked them which of his rare and priceless treasures had impressed them the most. It was the nightingale which they remembered.

"Not only does your bird sing more sweetly than any other," they said, "but it even sings for you at night, when all other songbirds are sleeping. If it looks as beautiful as it sounds, it must be the rarest creature in all the world."

Now the truth was that the Emperor had never even heard the nightingale, let alone seen it. But he did not want to show his ignorance.

"It is indeed the most exotic and colourful of all birds," he boasted. "It has been trained at vast expense to sing so beautifully by night. You are right to name it as the jewel of my kingdom."

As soon as the wise men had gone, he sent his servants into the forest to find the wondrous nightingale and bring it to him. They found him a handsome bird with a tail like a jewelled fan, but its shriek made the Emperor cover his ears. They found him a bird with bright green plumage, but it only squawked and kept imitating his royal commands in a most disrespectful way. They found him a bird with a crown on its head and tail feathers a yard long, but it did not seem to make any sound at all.

At last the servants were forced to tell the Emperor the awful truth. They brought him a plain brown little bird, sitting disconsolately in its wicker cage, and pressing their foreheads against the marble floor they murmured:

"Great Emperor, this wretched and unworthy creature is the nightingale you seek!"

The Emperor stared at the bird through narrowed eyes. "Then why does it not sing?" he asked in a voice like acid.

The courtiers pressed their heads even harder against the floor.

"It will not sing while it is caged," they croaked.

"Then set it free," said the Emperor.

With trembling fingers, the servants opened the cage and watched as the nightingale flew out through the palace window. There was a gasp of horror. But once outside, the bird perched upon the branch of a blossoming tree and began to sing.

As the clear notes drifted through the palace rooms, a great quietness fell over all the anxious courtiers. It seemed that every joy and sorrow in their hidden hearts found an echo in the beautiful sound. It spoke to them of things more precious than fine robes and jewelled baubles. Even the Emperor felt his heart touched. He forgot that he was a great emperor and remembered only that he was a man. As the final notes died away, two tears spilled over from his closed eyes and ran down his cheeks.

When he had recovered himself and remembered how important he was, he gave orders that the nightingale should have whatever reward she should ask for. The little bird flew close and perched upon the back of his throne.

"My lord," she said, "as you listened to my song, you shed two tears: they are reward enough for me."

The Emperor looked closely at the plain, brown bird: it had bright, intelligent eyes.

"Some nights," he said softly, "I cannot sleep. If you will sing to me in the long dark hours when my life seems meaningless, I will give you wealth beyond your wildest dreams."

"I have no need of wealth," said the nightingale, "yet I will come when you have need of me, for the sake of the two tears."

And so it was that the nightingale came to live in the palace gardens. Each night she sang to the Emperor when he could not sleep, and her sweet song soothed him and brought him great comfort.

Far away in Japan, the wise men returned and told their master of the great Emperor of China, with his splendid court and his marvellous singing bird. Now there was in Japan a most skilful craftsman who made wonderful mechanical toys. The Emperor of Japan ordered him to make a nightingale.

The craftsman asked the wise men what the bird looked like and how it sang. They managed to play for him on a flute some notes of the song, but as for its looks, they had never actually seen the bird. However they did not like to admit that.

"It is the most exotic and colourful bird in all the world," they told him. "Put in as many rubies and emeralds and diamonds as you can."

The craftsman brought to the Japanese Emperor a jewelled bird of surpassing beauty. It had bright eyes made of diamonds, sweeping tail feathers of rubies, and wings covered in emeralds which flapped as it sang. It sat on a perch inside a golden cage and in the jewelled base of the cage was the music box which made it sing.

The Emperor of Japan put the gold cage inside an inlaid ebony casket, wrapped it carefully in a cloth embroidered with pearls, and sent it to the Emperor of China.

When the gift arrived at the end of its long journey, it caused a great stir. In the presence of the Emperor, the ambassador unwrapped the treasure with great solemnity. There was a gasp of wonder at the sight of the jewelled bird. Then he carefully wound up the music box and the bird began to sing. It flapped its sparkling emerald wings; it opened and shut its shining gold beak and sweet fluting notes filled the room. The Emperor of China looked at the bright jewelled bird and was ashamed of his own drab, brown nightingale. He told the ambassador to thank his brother emperor for his magnificent gift and announced that henceforth the bird would be appointed Official Court Nightingale.

When she heard this, the real nightingale, who had seen everything from the tree outside the window, flew away back to the forest. She missed her old home and was pleased that the Emperor had found a new comfort for his sleepless nights.

At first, the Emperor was delighted with his new toy. But although its fluting notes were very like the real thing, it could sing only one brief song and this it sang over and over and over again. As the Emperor lay awake in the dark hours of the night, the repetition frayed his fragile nerves. He came to know each separate note and he felt the fall of each one like the drips of the water torture.

"Where is my real nightingale?" he roared in anguish: he remembered that she could sing all night long and never once repeat a phrase of her tune.

When his servants told him that the real nightingale had gone, he flew into a fury. "No one leaves the court except at my command!" he shouted. "I am the one who gives the orders. If the nightingale has gone, it is because I have banished her. Let her never be seen or heard near my palace again, upon pain of death!"

He spoke the words out of tiredness and anger, but they could not be unsaid without loss of face. And so the Emperor condemned himself to lie awake uncomforted through the long, dark hours of the night.

Without sleep he grew ever more tired; being always tired, he lost his appetite; without food, his strength failed; growing weak, he became ill; and finding no cure for his sickness, the shadow of death drew close to him.

His courtiers watched his decline with interest but without sorrow: they had feared him too much ever to have loved him. When they saw that he was dying, they stole away, one by one, and went to seek his cousin who would become the new Emperor. There would be rich pickings when the new heir took the throne and none of them wanted to lose his share.

Left alone in his sadness, the old Emperor called out in his feeble voice: "Alas, my sweet nightingale, I have such need of you now." And two tears spilled over from his closed eyes and ran down his cheeks.

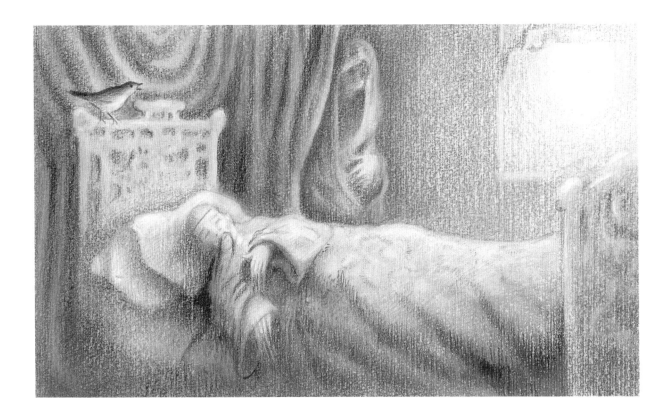

At once, the nightingale was beside him, for she had heard of his sickness and, risking death, had passed many nights silently watching outside his window. Now she perched on the head of his bed and began to sing to him.

The dying Emperor heard her sweet voice as if in a dream. It calmed his beating heart; it soothed his anxious mind; his tears ceased to flow and at last, he slept. The nightingale ended her song and gazed down at the sleeping man.

"Do not stop," said a voice from the darkness.

"Who speaks?" asked the nightingale. "I thought you had all gone to seek a better fortune."

A hooded figure stepped from the shadows and stood by the bedside. "I shall not leave," it said, "until I take him with me."

And the nightingale saw that it was Death.

"What need have you of my song?" she asked.

"It will be a tiresome wait," said Death, "and your sweet song pleases me."

"A musician must be paid," said the nightingale. Death laughed. "Name your price," he said.

"Why, my lord," said the nightingale softly, "my price is this old man's life."

"He is not a good man," said Death. "Why should you care?"

"Because he wept to hear me sing," said the nightingale. "Give him a little longer and he may yet die a good man."

"Will you sing for me until dawn?" asked Death.

"Until the cock crows," said the nightingale.

Death laughed again, a hollow, rattling laugh, and the bargain was sealed.

All night she sang, that plain brown bird, while the jewelled toy stared motionless from its diamond eyes, inside the silent cage of gold. And as she sang, the old man slept, a deep sleep that healed his heart and strengthened his weak body.

When the sun rose and the cock crew, Death moved silently away and the Emperor woke at last to find himself hungry. He struck the brass gong beside his bed and brought all the servants running. And the courtiers who waited for news of his death found themselves disappointed.

The Emperor grew strong and powerful again, but he never forgot that inside his gorgeous robes, he was a man like any other. He did his best to rule well and his people grew to love him.

But for the Emperor, his first love was always the little brown bird, and the song of the nightingale remained his greatest joy.

Giselle

Berthe stood at the window of her cottage and watched her daughter dance: it was a sight that always gave her pleasure. There was a lightness in the girl's feet and a joy in every step that gave to her dancing a special grace.

Berthe sighed, for that dancing was also her greatest worry. Giselle was a delicate child, yet she danced with a passion that tired her out. But she is not a child any more, she reminded herself. That was another worry.

A group of young men stood in the shade of the trees, watching the girls dance. She could see the gamekeeper, Hilarion, dark and frowning, his eyes fixed on Giselle. If only he were not so dour and quick-tempered. He was an honest man and devoted to her daughter, but his rough ways would never win the heart of a lively girl. Small wonder if Giselle preferred Loys with his gentle manners and his friendly charm . . . and, of course, with his handsome looks, she thought, smiling. Her anxious eyes sought his fair head, but he was not to be seen. And that's another thing, she thought, where does Loys get to, when he's not with Giselle? He was a newcomer to the village who now lived in a cottage close by, but they really knew very little about him. She sighed again; a widow's life was full of worries, especially when her only daughter was of an age to marry.

But Giselle had been dancing long enough and, moving to the doorway, Berthe called her daughter in.

Giselle came reluctantly but without arguing. She was flushed and breathless, and she needed a cool drink and a quiet rest in the shade of the kitchen.

"Feel how your heart is racing," said her mother anxiously, as she filled a mug with fresh milk from the pitcher. "One of these days you'll drop dead in the middle of the dance . . . and you know what will become of you then."

"Yes, Mother," Giselle smiled at her gently, her lip rimmed with the pale cream. "You are always telling me! I shall join the spirits of maidens who died before their wedding day. I shall drift about the forest clearings in a long, white dress and frighten the life out of harmless travellers."

Her mother frowned. "It is all very well for you to laugh," she said, "but many have seen the spirits and some did not live to tell the tale."

Giselle put down her glass and threw her arms around her mother. "Don't worry," she said, "I shan't become a dismal spirit. I shall marry –" she hesitated – "Some nice boy, and have a big happy family of grand-children for you to spoil."

"God grant that you may," said Berthe. "And I think I know who that young man will be."

Giselle blushed. She wondered if there was anyone in the whole village who did not know that she was in love with Loys. But what did that matter, she thought, since he loved her just as dearly. He had vowed it many times and soon, she was certain, he would ask her to name their wedding day.

Her face clouded for a moment as she remembered Hilarion's words that morning, some wicked tale that Loys was not what he seemed. The game-keeper had sworn that he had seen Loys with a rich cloak and carrying a jewelled sword. He claimed that both were hidden away in the young man's cottage. But Hilarion would say anything to separate us, she thought; he tells these lies to fill me with doubts. Loys would never deceive me; I would trust him with my life.

Outside, the dancing went on, as the village celebrated a good wine harvest. All morning Giselle had danced with Loys, unwilling to stop, even when she felt tired. But then his friend had called him aside, speaking in lowered tones, and Loys had returned to say that he must leave her for a while. She hated it when he went away, but he had promised her to return by evening, and it was true that she did need to rest for a while.

Then a sudden clamour of hunting horns sent her flying to the window. "Mother, come quickly," she called, "here is some great lord's hunting party, and a lady with them so fine she must be a princess! They are dismounting, Mother, and I think they mean to knock at our door!" Before Berthe could answer, Giselle was at the door herself, flinging it wide and inviting the strangers inside.

Her mother smiled and offered refreshments to the hunting party. The "great lord", who was in fact the prince of that land, thanked her and graciously accepted her hospitality. Their arrival had interrupted the villagers' dancing but his daughter, the Princess Bathilde, asked that it might continue for their entertainment.

"Oh, Mother, let me dance too," begged Giselle, "let me dance again for our guests."

"One dance only, then," said Berthe, "for the sun is hot and you are already tired."

Her daughter ran to join the other girls and, in the dappled shade of the trees, danced with a grace and skill that set her apart from her fellows. When the dance ended, the princess called to her and, unclasping her own gold chain, fastened it around the young dancer's neck. Giselle was quite overwhelmed with excitement and thought the princess the loveliest creature she had ever seen.

The prince chose to rest for a while in the cool of Berthe's cottage.

"Rouse us again with your horn," he told the huntsman, "when the hounds have scented a fresh quarry."

While they were inside, Loys returned and Giselle hurried out to meet him, moving quietly so as not to disturb their guests. She was longing to show him her golden chain and to tell him about the lovely princess. She ran to where he stood and he put his arms around her, but before she could speak a word, Hilarion appeared, his face twisted with anger.

"I have you now, Loys," he said, spitting out the name as if it were an insult, "though I think you are no more 'Loys' than I am."

Loys flushed and drew Giselle closer. "What nonsense is this?" he said.

Hilarion brought his hands from behind his back and held out a jewelled sword and a fine embroidered cloak. "I think these are yours," he said.

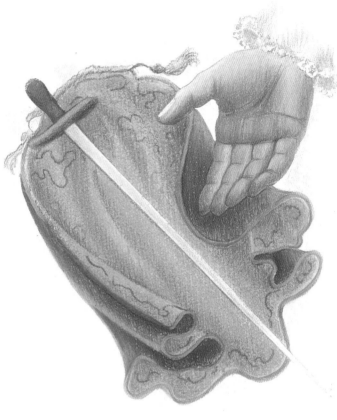

"Strange treasure for a simple peasant to keep hidden in his cottage."

"I know nothing of these," said Loys, but his voice was strained.

Giselle looked from one man to the other with frightened eyes.

"I think you do, my lord," said Hilarion softly, and his softness was more deadly than his rage. "These bear the crest of a nobleman and one who plays dishonourable games, I think, with this young girl's love."

Giselle felt her heart begin to race. She stepped back and gazed up at Loys. "Dear love," she pleaded, "tell me he is lying."

But Loys stood silent and his face was pale.

As the two men faced one another, a hunting horn rang out through the forest, startling them both. Then the door of Berthe's cottage opened and the prince and his daughter stepped out into the sunlight.

"Albrecht, how come you here?" The Princess Bathilde crossed to where Loys stood. "And why this peasant dress, my lord? Do you take part in the dancing?"

Loys knelt slowly before her and kissed her hand. "I had not looked to see you here, princess," he said.

"So it would seem." Bathilde's voice was amused. "I could almost suspect my betrothed of some intrigue."

Giselle was trembling; she could not keep her hands from shaking.

"Betrothed . . ." she stammered, and the words would hardly come. "Are you betrothed, lady?"

Bathilde held out her left hand on which shone a fine, jewelled ring. "Indeed, child," she said, "and to the Duke Albrecht whom you see before you," and she laid her hand upon Loy's arm.

"No! No!" Giselle felt as if her heart would stop from the pain of the blow. Tears sprang in her eyes and ran down her cheeks. She tore the gold chain from around her neck, and threw it to the ground.

The other girls ran to comfort her, but she pushed them away, running wildly from place to place like a trapped and hunted animal.

Berthe, coming out of the house, was horrified to see her daughter's stricken face and empty eyes. "What is this?" she cried. "What have you done to my child?"

And then Giselle began to dance. She moved slowly and sorrowfully, her eyes fixed and staring. At first the crowd stood back, hoping that she might find comfort in the familiar movements. But as she circled about, the dance grew faster and faster, wilder and ever more frantic, until Berthe cried out, "Stop! Stop, my darling, for pity's sake."

Then Giselle did stop, suddenly, like a stricken beast. Stumbling, she held out her arms towards Albrecht, towards the one who had always been her beloved Loys. But as he ran forward, her breaking heart failed her and she fell lifeless into his arms. At first it seemed to the onlookers that she had fainted, until they heard his despairing cry and saw Berthe's face, white with shock.

Then there was a great outpouring of grief. Weeping, Albrecht moved to carry Giselle's body into the shelter of her mother's house, but Hilarion seized it roughly out of his arms.

"You have no business here," he cried. "This is your doing, my lord. Leave us to bear our sorrow in our own way."

Albrecht could not deny the truth of his words. He turned aside, blinded by his tears, and rode with the prince and his party away out of the forest.

But he could not so easily leave behind his grief or his sense of wrong-doing. He passed a sleepless night and a day when he could not eat. The following night he rose by moonlight, saddled his horse and rode back through the forest. He seemed drawn by an irresistible power to the woodland glade where Giselle had been laid to rest.

Coming at dead of night through the moonlit shadows of the forest, he expected to find no other mourners at her graveside. But he had reckoned without Hilarion, whose conscience had driven him also to stand watch in that silent place.

The two men came face to face across the grave and even there, hatred flared between them. Each reached for his weapon but, before they could come to blows, both became aware of a strange force stirring through the forest. Pale lights flickered among the trees, moving and growing until each one took on the shape of a young girl in a flowing white dress. They seemed to be gathering around the grave and, though pale and beautiful, they felt threatening and full of power. Then both Albrecht and Hilarion knew that they stood in great danger.

One maiden, taller and sterner than the rest, seemed to rule among them. She called to Giselle and as the two men watched, they saw her pale spirit rise from the mound that marked her grave. Hilarion stepped forward and tried to take hold of her. But at once the vengeful spirits encircled him. He found himself caught up by an overwhelming force which carried him away helplessly through the dark forest. His cries and struggles were useless. The power was like a whirlwind, sweeping him down to the

lakeside where the waters rose up to meet it. He felt himself falling into a roaring funnel of water which sucked him down into its depths, drowning forever his last cry of despair.

In the clearing by the grave, Giselle and Albrecht came together again. He held out his arms to the spirit of his lost love and moved with her as if in a last dance, trying to recall the happiness they had shared. But he too was to feel the vengeance of the spirits. With Hilarion dead, they now gathered about Albrecht, seeking to drag him to the same fate.

But Giselle clung to him and would not let him go. Her love was stronger than the hatred of the spirits and, while she danced with him, they could not tear Albrecht away from her. When the queen of the spirits saw that Giselle resisted her, she sought to turn her love against her. Since she could not part them, she compelled the lovers to dance ever faster and more wildly. The spirit Giselle could dance for ever without tiring, but she knew that her lover's mortal body could not stand the strain. She saw that he would dance to his death.

In Giselle's gentle heart, there was no place for vengeance. Though Albrecht had deceived her, she loved him still and she would not let him die. As she led him by the hand in their wild dance, she drew him ever closer to the simple wooden cross that marked her grave. She knew that once he touched it, he would be safe from the spirits. Dizzy and breathless, his life ebbing, Albrecht threw out a despairing hand and grasped the cross. At once the wild dance faded; he fell face down upon the grave, and blackness engulfed him.

When he opened his eyes again, dawn was breaking. The first birds sang in the misty forest, and the terrible spirits were gone. Then Albrecht knew that there is a love that is greater than hatred, a love which can survive both deceitfulness and death. But he knew also that to each man such a love comes only once, and that it would be his fate to live out the rest of his life without it.

Coppelia

Swanilda came into the village square, looking for her boyfriend Franz. She was also looking for a quarrel.

Franz had been courting her for nearly a year. Each day, without fail, he had called at her house to take her walking beside the stream, or dancing at a village fête, or simply to hold her hand and swear his undying love. He had won her parents' approval, they had named the wedding day: and now this had happened!

Yesterday she had waited all day long and he had not come at all. Instead, a girl she had never really liked had stopped by, especially to tell her that Franz had a new love.

"She's the daughter of old Dr Coppelius," said the girl, "and she's very, very beautiful. All the boys are wild about her, but your Franz is the one she seems to like best."

At first Swanilda tossed her head and refused to believe her. After all, it was not very likely that the toymaker would suddenly acquire a daughter, let alone a beautiful one. He was old and ugly, and bad-tempered too. He had always lived alone in his crooked house in the village square. The local people kept away from him, and told tall stories about what went on in the old house, from which came sounds of creaking and hammering at all hours of the day and night.

But this evening, when Franz still had not come, Swanilda had decided to see for herself. Now she paused behind one of the trees that lined the square, and looked across at the old man's window. It was true! There, in full view, sat a girl with a pale face and long dark hair. Her head was bent, as if over some needlework, and she was certainly very beautiful.

Swanilda watched as several of the village boys passed by and waved to the newcomer. The girl turned her head and smiled gently each time, before returning to her work. Then Franz came round the corner and paused to gaze up at the window. This time the girl raised her hand as well, and waved as she smiled. Franz seemed delighted and blew kisses in return before he went on his way.

"The rat! The snake!" thought Swanilda angrily. "Wait till I get my hands on him! And as for that scheming creature, if she thinks she can steal my Franz . . ." And she began to plan some terrible revenge.

She had not got very far with it when she saw old Dr Coppelius come out of his house. He closed the crooked door, locked it with a big brass key, and turned to go down the street. But as he went, two small boys came charging around the corner and bumped into him, knocking his walking stick from under him. The big key went flying through the air; it glinted in the sunlight and fell close to Swanilda's feet. The old man was so busy retrieving his stick that he did not notice the key.

He shouted after the boys, waved his stick angrily, and went on his way. Swanilda picked up the key and looked at it thoughtfully.

Just then several of her girlfriends came chattering along the street. They were all talking indignantly about the new girl. They said that her name was Coppelia and that she had been flirting with all their boyfriends. "Your Franz is as bad as all the rest," they told her, "and he's the one she's got her eye on!"

"Oh, has she!" said Swanilda scowling. "We'll soon see about that." And she marched across the square to where the girl had been sitting. But there was no sign of her now.

"Hey there! Coppelia!" called Swanilda, and the other girls joined in. But there was no answer. The house stood dark and silent.

"Well, that's typical!" said one of the girls. "She simpers and waves to all the boys, but when we call her, she doesn't want to know!"

Swanilda looked at the key in her hand. "She may not want to know us," she said, "but I think we will go and visit her." And she told them how she had come by the key to the old man's house.

"Would you dare to go in?" breathed one of the girls anxiously. "I mean, you hear such tales about the goings-on in that house."

"Well, if you are scared, I'm not," said Swanilda. Actually, she was rather nervous, but she really loved Franz and she wasn't going to give him up without a fight. "Come on," she said as she put the brass key into the lock.

Inside, the crooked house was dark and shuttered. Only an occasional thin beam of sunlight penetrated its dusty shadows.

It seemed to the nervous girls that strange shapes lurked in the corners, motionless but threatening. Several of them wanted to go back, but the bolder ones urged them on. "Upstairs," hissed Swanilda. "The girl is up there and I want to talk to her."

At the top of the stairs there was a little more light, from the half-curtained window where Coppelia had been sitting. The sunlight revealed looming life-sized figures: a Harlequin, a Juggler, a Pierrot, and many more. All stood quite still, their arms and legs frozen in awkward positions. Cautiously, Swanilda stretched out a finger and touched the Juggler. He moved suddenly, making all the girls jump and shriek. Then the figure was still again. Swanilda looked at it more closely and found a large key in the middle of its back. She turned it twice and at once the Juggler sprang to life, tossing and catching brightly coloured balls.

"Why, they are just big clockwork dolls," she said delightedly. Then she had a thought. Searching about, she found an alcove screened by a curtain. She pulled the curtain aside, and there sat the lovely Coppelia, silent and still. Feeling behind her, Swanilda found another key. She turned it, laughing as she did so, and at once the girl began to smile and wave to them.

As they realized that their rival, who had caused them so much heartache, was only a clockwork doll, the other girls began to laugh. They laughed even more as they thought what fools the boys had been, mooning over a big doll with their sighs and kisses. In the end, they laughed so much that they grew reckless: they ran about, winding up the other dolls until they all danced and juggled and waved their arms together. Then, just as things were getting really out of hand, they heard a cry of rage and, turning, saw the figure of Dr Coppelius standing in the doorway.

The laughter died as the girls froze in their places. Only the clockwork figures jerked and twitched their mechanical limbs, until even they grew still. For a long moment there was an uneasy silence; then the old man gave a sudden roar and rushed forward, waving his stick. The girls fled around him and away down the stairs, squeaking with fear like mice in an attic. Only Swanilda remained, trapped on the far side of the room. Looking frantically about her, she dived into Coppelia's alcove and quickly whisked the curtain back into place.

The old man shut out the sun, then growled and muttered in the darkness. He lit a lamp and moved about the room, looking to see if his figures were damaged. He did not seem to like the daylight. When at last he reached the alcove, he drew back the curtain to inspect his beloved Coppelia. He thought she looked rather untidy as he moved the lamp closer. Her wig was askew and he straightened it carefully.

But before he could examine her more closely, there was a sound at the window. The old man blew out his lamp and, silent as a ghost, drew back into the shadows. A moment later the shutter creaked open, and Franz climbed over the windowsill into the room.

Thinking himself alone, he called softly to Coppelia, and was startled when the old man's voice replied: "And what business have you with my daughter, that brings you here like a thief to my house?"

Caught out, Franz could only tell the truth. "Forgive me, Doctor," he said, "it was wrong, I know. But my love for your daughter has made me reckless."

"So, you love my daughter, do you?" The old man's voice cackled with amusement. "Then perhaps you will be glad to do her a little service?"

"Anything you ask!" said Franz eagerly.

"Then sit down, young man," said the toymaker, "and let us see how much you care for her."

Franz was delighted to find himself made welcome. The old man re-lit the lamp, fetched a bottle, and poured his visitor a glass of wine. It had a strange, bitter taste, but Franz hardly noticed it. Perhaps he is anxious to find a husband for his lovely daughter, he thought hopefully. But even as the thought passed through his head, he felt himself grow dizzy and confused. He had only just time to realize that the wine was drugged, before he pitched face downward on the table and fell into a deep sleep.

"Now for that small service for which you were so willing." The old man seemed to gloat over poor Franz. "I shall use your useless spirit to give life to my lovely child."

He took down a great Book of Magic from a dusty shelf and, laying it open upon the table, began to chant one of the spells inside. As he did so, he waved his bony hands in the air, as if trying to draw the very life force out of Franz and pass it into the doll he had created. And it seemed that the magic was working! As he watched, he saw Coppelia yawn and stretch her arms, as if waking from a long sleep.

But the doll was really Swanilda, who had disguised herself in Coppelia's clothes and her dark wig. Moving stiffly, she rose from her chair and marched about the room. At first, she followed the old toymaker's commands, but soon, much to his dismay, she seemed to take on a will of her own. She rushed around, crashing into his precious toys, breaking their arms and legs. Then she began to dance, whirling around the room, and each time she passed Franz she paused for a moment and shook him hard, trying to wake him up.

In the dark, shadowy room, the old man was in despair. He had given his Coppelia the gift of life. He had turned her from a mechanical doll into a breathing, living girl, and now, it seemed, she was completely out of control.

Franz was beginning to wake up, and he was equally dismayed to see the quiet, delicate Coppelia behaving like a mad thing. Around she went again, spinning past him. Crash! The lamp went flying and the light went out.

Someone was pulling him to his feet; someone was dragging him away down the stairs. Franz went willingly: he had had quite enough of the toymaker's daughter.

Back in the room, the old man struggled to rekindle the lamp. As the faint light flared, he gazed around upon a scene of terrible destruction, all his beautiful dolls smashed to pieces. But at least Coppelia seemed to have lost her power of movement, and now lay motionless on the floor of the alcove. Her clothes were scattered about and her wig seemed to be missing; but that was a small price to pay, he thought, for peace and quiet. Shaking his head in bewilderment, the old man vowed to himself that he would stick to his toy-making, and never dabble in magic again.

Outside in the darkening street, Swanilda walked home with a rather confused Franz. He was not at all sure what she was grumbling about, or why she kept thumping him every now and then. But he was very grateful to be free of the wild, crazed Coppelia, and to have his old love back again. Whatever he had done, he thought, Swanilda would forgive and forget tomorrow.

Swan Lake

 T here once lived a queen who fell foul of an enchanter. It happened so long ago that no one can remember the cause of their quarrel, just as no one can forget the tragedy of his revenge.

Seeking about for what would hurt her most, the Enchanter's eye fell upon the queen's young daughter, playing among her maidens. He summoned his magic powers and turned the laughing girls into a flock of white swans whose whiteness and beauty alone bore witness to their true nature.

The queen was quite broken by his cruelty, and until the day of her death, she never ceased to weep for her loss. Her salt tears flowed down and gathered into a dark lake, as deep and bottomless as her grief. And it was in this lake, when she could bear her sorrow no longer, that the sad queen drowned herself.

Long years passed; tall trees grew up all around; and still the princess and her maidens, ageless and immortal while the spell lay upon them, swam like white swans upon the lake of tears.

And then, at last, a young prince chanced upon the place. Hunting with his friends, he had out-ridden them all and found himself alone in a dark forest.

Night was falling. The trees were dense and overgrown, and at first he could find no path to follow. Then, seeing a gleam of light ahead, he made his way towards it, and came out on the shores of a wide lake which shone like silver in the moonlight.

Swimming upon the surface of the water, he saw a flock of white swans and his first instinct, as a hunter, was to raise his crossbow and take aim. But something about the beauty of the birds, and the strangeness of finding them there at night, when most birds are sleeping, made him think again. He stepped back into the shadow of a tree and wondered why the sight of them seemed to disturb his heart. Then, as he watched, the white birds swam towards the shore, and each in turn raised her white wings into the air and changed into a beautiful young girl. As the last swan came close, the prince saw that she wore a tiny coronet of pearls upon her white head. And when she too was transformed, he knew that he had found the princess of his dreams.

He stepped out from behind the tree, moving carefully so as not to startle her. But when the swan maiden saw him, she held out her arms without fear and ran lightly towards him.

"At last," she breathed . . . "at last there is hope for us all."

Then, taking the prince by the hand and gazing up at him with her wide dark eyes, she told him the sad tale of their enchantment. As she reached the end of her story she wept, saying:

"Only for this little time each night does the Enchanter restore our human form, and then only lest we should forget who we are and so cease to grieve."

The prince could not bear the sight of her tears.

"Tell me how the spell may be broken," he begged. "Whatever the price may be, I will pay it."

"The spell can only be broken by one who will love me with all his heart," said the swan princess, "one who will swear to marry me and who will never break faith."

"Why then, that is easy," said the prince joyfully. "You have my heart already, and I will take no other bride."

As he spoke, the moon passed behind a cloud; a cold wind sprang up, and the bright mirror of the lake turned to grey steel.

The prince shivered with a sudden sense of foreboding, and the swan maidens cowered as a dark shadow passed overhead.

Throwing his arms around the swan princess, holding her close to protect her, the prince felt her heart beat against him like a trapped bird.

"It is the Enchanter!" she whispered. "He comes each night like a great black owl, to watch us change back into swans. It gives him a cruel pleasure to feel his power over us."

The prince took hold of his crossbow.

"Let him come tonight," he said angrily, "and I will tear him out of the sky!"

"No!" cried the princess, "that you must never do! Only he can release us from the spell. His death would be our disaster."

She drew away from him as she spoke, and the prince saw that all the swan maidens were moving back towards the water. They walked like dreamers, with heads bowed, and he saw that some great power was over them.

"Do not fail me," begged the swan princess, turning as she reached the water's edge. "Meet me here again tomorrow night."

"I will not fail!" said the prince, and he watched with an aching heart as she raised her white arms for a moment and became once more a swan upon the water.

Swiftly he rode home through the night, but could find no sleep when he reached his bed. Rising early next day, he found all the palace in great confusion and remembered with a sinking heart that this was the day of his coming of age. There was to be a great ball that night to which would be invited all the most eligible princesses from the lands round about.

And I am supposed to choose from among them, he thought, a partner to share my life and, one day, my throne. He laughed at the thought. That would never be, for he could only love one woman. He could not tell his parents this strange story of a swan princess; he knew that they would never believe him. No, he told himself, I have no choice but to go through with this charade, but I shall refuse each one. Nothing shall ever separate me from my true love.

The day seemed endless, but at last he dressed himself in his finest clothes and, sad at heart, went to the ball.

There were six princesses and, as the evening wore on, the prince danced with them all. Some were proud and pretty, others were proud and plain. One seemed beautiful and kind, and the prince thought, In another life, I might have loved her. But always the dark pleading eyes of the swan princess came between him and the smiling faces. He could not wait for the ball to end, so that he could escape to the pale lake in the dark forest.

Then the queen took him aside and asked him to choose a bride from among the six princesses.

"Mother, I cannot," he said. "Would you have me choose, by looks alone, a girl I hardly know? These things need time." And yet he knew that he had loved the swan princess at first sight.

Before the queen could answer, there was a sudden commotion in the palace courtyard, a rattling of carriage wheels and a wild neighing of horses.

The doors of the ballroom were flung open and into the room strode a tall and striking man, in a cloak of swirling darkness. A cold wind came with him, and the prince caught the scent of pine trees and the dank smell of stagnant waters. But this frightening apparition led by the hand quite a different vision: a princess who, in spite of her splendid black and silver dress, bore the unmistakable features of his own dear swan princess.

The prince could hardly believe his eyes. The face he knew, there was no mistaking it; and yet her manner was haughty, her eyes triumphant.

"Madam," said the tall man to the queen, "I bring you a princess worthy of your son, and one, I think, whom he will not refuse."

The prince led the new princess into the dance.

"My love, is it truly you?" he whispered. "What brings you here, and in such company?"

"It is the Enchanter who has brought me to you," whispered the princess. "Seeing us by the lakeside and hearing you pledge your love, he knew that you were destined to break his spell. Therefore, knowing that you will one day rule in this land, he now seeks your friendship." As she spoke, she smiled and gazed up at him with her wide, dark eyes.

But the prince was strangely uneasy: it seemed to him that he danced with a different girl. The eyes were knowing and flashed fire like the rich diamonds on her black dress. He felt a sense of loss, remembering the gentle eyes which had gazed into his own by the lakeside. "Am I indeed pledged to this hard, bright creature," he wondered, "or is this some trick of the Enchanter?"

The princess seemed to read his thoughts.

"Ah, my love," she whispered, "do not fail me. I fear that the Enchanter puts doubts into your mind, making me seem other than my true self. He stakes everything on this last throw, knowing that if you deny me now, I am lost forever."

"That shall never be," said the prince. "You have my promise and I will not be forsworn."

The dark eyes with their hard glitter held his as a snake holds its prey. He did not see the skein of white swans passing across the night sky beyond the ballroom window.

"Then let all hear your promise," said the princess, smiling up at him with the face he loved. "Pledge yourself to me, so that the spell may be broken and our happiness begin." Her voice was low, but there was no gentleness in it.

The prince summoned all his courage, determined that the Enchanter's tricks should not make him deny his swan princess. "Once the spell is broken," he thought, "she will be my own dear love again."

Taking her by the hand, he led the princess to where his parents sat enthroned.

"Behold," he said, "I have made my choice. This maiden and no other shall be my bride."

At once the Enchanter was beside him.

"Let him swear," he said, "before all this company. Let him swear to this marriage and if he fails, let his life be forfeit."

As his dark cloak swirled about him, the prince caught again the smell of dank things, rotting in nameless depths. Once more he was filled with doubt.

"Ah!" cried the princess, gazing up at him with her lovely face. "Has he turned you against me? It is as I feared!" She lowered her head, covering her face with her hands, and it seemed to him that she wept.

The prince took her in his arms.

"I swear," he cried, "that I will wed this princess, or forfeit my life."

As he spoke, he heard a terrible sound at the high window. All heads turned, all eyes were raised to see a white swan that beat its wings frantically against the glass.

Then the prince knew that he had been deceived. He looked down at the girl in his arms and, as she raised her head, saw with horror that she bore quite another face, a face with eyes that mocked and a mouth twisted in scorn.

Thrusting her away from him, he ran from the ballroom, with the harsh sound of her laughter ringing in his ears. Outside in the cold night, he seized a horse from a waiting groom and rode desperately towards the swan lake. As he rode, he saw ahead of him the white birds, passing across the moon. He reached the lake as they landed, and watched as they changed once more into human form. As the swan princess stepped from the water, the prince gathered her into his arms and held her against his heart.

"Forgive me," he said, "for believing for one moment that that foul creature could be you."

"She is his daughter," said the swan princess. "He used his magic power to give her my face." She spoke no word of reproach, but the prince cursed himself for being deceived.

"What can be done," he asked, "to undo this harm? How can I save you now?"

"Do not blame yourself," said the swan princess gently. "The cunning of the

Enchanter runs too deep for honest hearts to fathom. Soon he will come like a dark owl, to feast himself on our grief. When he comes this time, you must destroy him."

"But if I do," said the prince, "the spell can never be broken."

"If you do not," said the swan princess, "Your own life will be forfeit."

"How can I leave you forever beneath the spell of that evil man?"

"Ah, do not fear," said the princess, "it lies in my own power to end my enchantment. Before this night ends, I shall go to join my mother in her deep lake of tears. Long has she called to me and always I have answered, 'Wait but a little longer, Mother, for there is still hope.' Now all hope is gone, and my only escape lies in her arms." Even as she spoke, the wind sprang up, the mirror of the lake clouded, and a monstrous shadow passed overhead. Then, in his despair, the prince raised his bow, drew back the bolt, and brought the dark enemy crashing out of the sky.

Side by side the lovers stood, gazing upon the twisted body of the great owl. The shape shifted as they watched, and the Enchanter lay dead at their feet.

Then the swan princess kissed the prince for the last time. "You are safe now," she said, "and my sorrow will soon be ended."

The prince saw that the swan maidens were becoming swans again. He clung to the princess as she moved towards the water, but she said:

"My love you must let me go. Never again can I take human form. My maidens will live as swans forever and will soon forget what they have been. But for me, having once known your love, it would be an eternity of grief. If you love me, let me go to my mother before it is too late."

Weeping, the prince released her, and watched as she walked out into the water. She moved without hesitating and without looking back, until the lake of tears closed over her head.

Then the prince turned his back upon the cold shore where the dead Enchanter lay, and walked blindly away into the forest. He knew now that he was safe, that he was free to return to the palace and to take up his life again, as if the swan maiden had never been. He thought of the princess who had seemed kind and beautiful: how happy his parents would be if he could take her as his bride.

The path wound about bringing him out on to a high cliff above the lake. He turned back to gaze for the last time upon those dark waters. A storm now raged with terrible power, whipping the waves into a wild fury, and it seemed to him that he heard in the wind the voice of his love, calling to him. Suddenly he knew that without her, his life would be no more than an empty shell. The sorrow and the loneliness seemed more than he could bear. He wanted only to rejoin his lost love in whatever world she might now be. With a great cry, he leaped from the cliff edge out into the darkness, and fell towards the angry waves surging below.

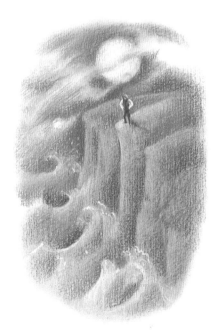

Petrushka

It was quite black inside the box. There was not the smallest chink of light, once the lid was closed and the latch was fastened. But Petrushka did not mind the darkness, indeed at times he found it quite comforting.

He spent most of his life in the box. Once the show was over, the puppet master wasted no time. As the curtain fell to the applause of the crowd and the laughter of children, the smile would vanish from the old man's face. He scowled at the limp puppets which were his stock-in-trade, looking them over for signs of wear and tear. The gold braid was coming loose on the Moor's red jacket; that would have to be fixed. There was a small tear in the Ballerina's net skirt where it had been caught on the Moor's sword; that would need mending. As for the clown, Petrushka, his wooden face was so worn, and his baggy suit so tattered, that he would soon have to be replaced altogether. Into their boxes they went, down came the lids, and the latches clicked into place.

Alone in the darkness, Petrushka listened to the sounds of the stage being taken down and packed away. He felt the jolt as the boxes were tossed up on to the cart, and then the steady rumbling of wheels on the cobblestones as the puppet show moved on to another town.

Life was much simpler inside the box. The pain and the sadness did not go away, but at least there was nothing he could do about it. And always, as he thought about his life, he managed to persuade himself that things would be different next time.

He shivered as he thought of the fierce and handsome Moor. But it's not his fault that he is so frightening, he thought; it's just the part he has to play.

Still, that was not much comfort when the Moor danced about the stage, whirling his wooden sword about his head and sweeping its blade within an inch of poor Petrushka's heart.

I shouldn't mind so much if only the Ballerina didn't love him, he thought. Why must she sit upon his knee and smile her lovely smile at him? As he thought of the Ballerina, with her golden hair and her round, blue eyes and her rosy cheeks, the pain in his heart was almost more than he could bear. But it would be different next time, he told himself. Suddenly, she would see how much he loved her; suddenly, she would confess that she loved him in return. He gave a big sigh as he imagined

how sweet their life would be together. Then, in the gently rocking darkness, he fell asleep.

He woke with a start as the wooden box was thrown down on to the stage: at once his heart began to race. The rumbling had stopped, and he could hear muffled sounds of music and laughter. It sounded like a big fairground, which was good. That meant a big audience and more money, and that would put the puppet master in a better mood.

As the lid of the box flew open, the sudden light seemed dazzling after the close darkness. Petrushka felt himself snatched up, and a moment later he was standing once more in his place on the stage, waiting for the dusty curtains to open. He just had time to glance sideways, to see his beloved Ballerina poised upon tiptoe in the centre of the stage, with the fierce Moor on the far side of her. Then the curtains swept back, he saw the crowd of staring faces, and the show had begun.

First the Ballerina danced daintily on the tips of her toes. Holding her hands above her head, she pirouetted about the stage, and all the little girls in the audience longed to be just like her. Petrushka knelt at the front of the stage and stretched out his arms pleadingly towards her. But she twirled past and hardly seemed to notice him.

She is not really so cruel, thought the unhappy clown; it is just the part she has to play on stage, just as I must always play the sad clown. It was not a difficult part for him to play, loving her as he did. The audience never knew that the tears he shed were real.

The Ballerina came to rest at the back of the stage, and the Moor leaped into the centre. How fine he looked, with the gold braid gleaming on his red coat and the silver paint flashing as he brandished his wooden sword! All the little boys in the audience, and some of their fathers too, wished that they could look so splendid and so bold.

46

Then the Moor blew kisses to the Ballerina. Shyly, she tiptoed towards him and as he knelt before her, she sat upon his knee. The crowd cheered and the Ballerina blew kisses to the audience.

If only she would send one kiss to me! thought Petrushka. One little kiss would be enough, but she never even looks my way. He crept closer and closer until he could reach out and touch her hand.

Startled, she gave a little cry, and the fierce Moor turned at the sound, fixing his dark, glowing eyes upon the pleading clown. He leapt angrily to his feet, upsetting the little Ballerina, which always made the audience laugh. Then he sprang towards Petrushka, whirling his sword about the unfortunate clown who cowered at the front of the stage. This was all part of the show, but it was the moment which Petrushka always dreaded. Every time, he thought that one day the sword would come too close and would put an end to his misery.

And now it happened at last. The floor of the stage was rough and worn, and the Moor's foot caught against a splinter. He tripped, then quickly regained his footing. But in that brief moment the sword caught the worn fabric of Petrushka's body. It split open, spilling sawdust across the stage, as the puppet master swiftly brought down the curtain.

Petrushka lay on the stage in a heap of sawdust. As his eyes grew dim, he watched the Moor and the Ballerina being picked up and put away in their boxes. Then the puppet master looked down at him. "Well, we shall certainly need a new clown now," he muttered, and with his foot he pushed poor Petrushka over the edge of the stage, where he fell into the darkness. The stage was taken down, the boxes were loaded, and the cart rumbled away into the night.

Petrushka listened as the sounds died away. So, this is how my life ends, he thought sadly, but he was too weak to move.

And then, just at that moment, a little girl came by. Tired and sleepy after a long day at the fair, she trailed behind her mother who held her firmly by the hand. She was a pretty child with golden curls, and round blue eyes, and rosy cheeks. She stopped as she saw the old, shabby puppet lying in the dust. She caught hold of his tattered clown suit and, picking him up, tucked him safely under her arm.

Gazing upwards in the dim light, Petrushka saw blue eyes that looked down with kindness, and a sweet mouth that smiled at him. He could not decide whether he was indeed in heaven, or whether he had just found a new part to play.

The Boy and the Magic

This is a story about a boy who was really naughty. He started out as a perfectly ordinary little boy, no better and no worse than you are. Then one day he got cross about something, and that made everyone angry with him, and then things just went from bad to worse.

He was rude to his mother, yelling at her and poking out his tongue, and though she loved him dearly, she felt that he must be punished before he grew even worse. She gave him dry bread for his supper: so he smashed the plate. She made him do sums instead of playing: so he tore up his book. He threw such a temper tantrum that his poor mother was in despair. She locked him up in the nursery and left him to see the error of his ways.

Left alone, he was really bad. Shouting and roaring, he smashed up the cups, and the teapot, and threw the kettle on to the floor. Yelling and screaming, he tore up his books, stopped the clock, and ripped the wallpaper off the wall. He pulled the cat's tail, sending her flying up the curtains; and just to prove how mean he could be, he teased the gentle squirrel which was his favourite pet. But then he felt so bad about what he had done, that he burst into tears and buried his face in the cushions of the armchair. When at last his angry sobs died away, there was a long silence in the room.

By now, the boy was frightened. He hardly dared look up to see the damage he had done. What would his father say when he came home? What punishment would be bad enough for him? Would his parents stop loving him because he was so bad?

And then a strange thing happened: he felt his armchair begin to move. At first, he thought that he had imagined it; then he opened his eyes and found that it was true. The armchair was walking about on its little stubby legs. Then he noticed that the tall grand-father clock said half past thirteen and that it was moving towards him.

He jumped down from the armchair and looked about him anxiously. A row of damaged teacups followed the cracked teapot to the edge of the table and they all jumped down onto the floor. The wallpaper had a pattern of shepherds and shepherdesses who were making their way down the torn strips, followed by their sheep.

Out from one of the damaged books came a fairytale princess; she looked sad and lonely, as if she had lost her home.

The boy rubbed his eyes in disbelief, and looked around at his other books which lay scattered across the floor. There were sums with arms and legs climbing out of his torn maths book, and maps with feet and faces slipping out from between the pages of his damaged atlas. The room was becoming very crowded, and the strange creatures who filled it seemed angry and threatening. The squirrel was nowhere to be seen, but the cat seemed much larger than before, and she was sharpening her fierce claws on the table leg.

They were all coming towards him now, and he knew that they meant to treat him as cruelly as he had treated them. The door was locked; he could not escape that way. He ran to the window and threw it open. There were prickly bushes outside, but the creatures were almost upon him. Closing his eyes, he leapt out of the window into the darkness.

The bushes scratched his face and hands, but at least they broke his fall. Never before had he been alone in the garden at night, and as he moved away across the moonlit lawn, it seemed to him a magical place. A night breeze made the trees sway; small bats danced like dark butterflies about his head; and frogs sang their serenade to the moon among the sleeping waterlilies. It was a world of quiet harmony and he longed to be part of it.

But then he noticed that the cat had come after him, and that there were other animals, fierce wild animals, prowling about in the night garden. He remembered how he had teased the cat and tormented the squirrel, and he knew that they had come to punish him. It seemed that there was no escape from his own wickedness. The moonlit garden darkened, a cold wind sprang up, and it became a place of nightmare.

The shapes of the animals grew bigger and more frightening. He called for his mother, but she could not hear him. Only the squirrel heard his familiar voice and, though he had treated it badly, it came leaping lightly down from its refuge in the tree-tops. But as it crossed the lawn, the wild animals all rushed at the boy and the little squirrel vanished under their pounding feet and claws.

The boy heard its cry and, forgetting his own danger, ran into the midst of the wild things. Braving the fangs and the claws, he picked up the wounded squirrel, and held it close to protect it from more danger.

At once, the wild animals seemed to grow quiet. They moved around him wonderingly as they saw his kindness to the little creature, and then they vanished silently away into the dark bushes. The boy carried the injured squirrel back into the house.

As he bandaged its paw with his handkerchief, he became aware of quiet movements in the room around him. Glancing up he saw that the shepherds and shepherdesses were driving their sheep back up the wallpaper and that they were pulling up the torn strips behind them as they went. The princess disappeared into the book of fairy stories, closing the cover carefully behind her. The sums were climbing back into the maths book, mending the tears as they went, and the maps were straightening out the atlas.

As he fed the frightened squirrel the remains of his supper bread, he noticed that the cups and the teapot were back on the table, and were using their tiny hands to fit their broken pieces into place. The kettle was back on the hob by the fire and was beginning to murmur softly. The cat had curled up in front of the fire and was purring like the kettle.

As he folded his warm jumper, and made a soft bed for the squirrel to sleep on, he noticed that the clock showed the right time again and that the armchair no longer moved on its stubby little legs. Tired and weary, his anger forgotten, the boy climbed back on to the comforting cushions and fell asleep.

It was there that his parents found him, when his father came home. "He looks so peaceful," he said affectionately, picking up his sleeping child.

"Yes," said his mother. "He did have a temper tantrum earlier, but he's a good boy really." And they carried him upstairs and tucked him quietly into his bed.

The Girl Who
Needed Watching

There was once a girl who needed watching. Everyone told her mother so.

"She's very lively," said the village midwife when Lise was born; "you'll have to watch her."

The mother said that she would.

"She's very clever," said the village teacher, when Lise was old enough to go to school; "you'll need to watch her."

The mother said that she did.

"She's very pretty," said the village priest, when Lise was seventeen; "you'll have to watch her very carefully."

The mother sighed and said that she never took her eyes off her daughter.

It was plain to all the village that if a girl was pretty and clever and lively, then she definitely needed watching. And they never let her mother forget it.

Lise found it all very tiresome; but it did not really become a problem until she fell in love. By this time her mother was a widow. She had a rich and prosperous farm and Lise was her only child. The farm next door was

also rich and prosperous: it belonged to a widower named Tomas who had an only son. The two neighbours agreed that their children should marry. The two farms could then become one and they would be richer and more prosperous than ever.

"But, Mother," said Lise when she heard of their plan, "I don't want to marry Alain."

"Young girls are always shy," said the widow; "you'll soon get used to the idea."

"But, Mother," said Lise, "he is as thin as a hayrake, as clumsy as a cow in a kitchen, and he has less to say for himself than a barnyard hen."

"Oh, he'll soon grow out of that," said her mother. She was quite fond of the young man. She had known him since he was a boy and had watched him growing up alone with his father. She thought there was nothing wrong with him that a bit of mothering wouldn't put right.

"But, Mother, he won't grow out of it," wailed Lise, "he's already twenty-four!" But the widow was not listening.

"Time you were in bed, dear," she said. "Give me a kiss and up you go."

Lise gave her a peck on the cheek, stamped off upstairs and slammed the bedroom door. Her mother sighed and wondered what girls were coming to. Once she is married, she thought, I shan't have to watch her all the time. It is such a worry: the only time I can take my eyes off her is when she is safely shut up in her bedroom.

In her bedroom, Lise sat by the window and thought how difficult mothers were. She had no intention of marrying Alain because she was in love with someone else. Colas was handsome, cheerful and hardworking.

He worked on the widow's farm and had no money except what he earned. Lise knew that her mother would not approve of the match; and that she might send him away if she knew of their love.

Because the widow watched her all the time, the love affair was little more than a few stolen glances, a few impatient sighs, and an occasional note passed from hand to hand. Colas was always looking for some excuse to come to the farmhouse kitchen. Then, for a few moments, he could watch his love as she worked, marvelling as her skilful hands churned butter, or kneaded bread, or rolled pastry. That morning Lise had managed to slip him a note telling him to come at dusk to her window. She knew that only in her bedroom was she safe from her mother's prying eyes. Now she saw him making his way through the orchard, dodging from tree to tree.

When she told him about the planned marriage, Colas turned pale. But Lise did not let him suffer for too long. "It's all right," she whispered. "Nothing will ever make me marry that tongue-tied beanpole."

"But he is very rich," said Colas miserably.

"So am I," said Lise, "and it would be greedy to have two farms when one will do."

Colas gazed at her admiringly, and wondered yet again how any girl could be so pretty and so lively and so clever.

"Don't worry," she told him, "I will think of a way. But go now before my mother comes out to shut up the hens."

Colas sadly did as he was told, turning back as he went to catch a last glimpse of his love, waving at him from the window.

The next day the widower brought his son to pay a formal visit. Alain was nearly as reluctant as Lise. He did not want to marry this pretty, lively, clever girl. He always felt plain, dull and stupid when he was with her, even when she tried to be kind. He did not really want a wife at all: what he wanted was a mother.

The widow suggested that they should all drive in her pony cart down to the harvest field. They could take a picnic and join the harvesters for their lunch. This would give the young couple a chance to get to know each other better, while she and Tomas kept an eye on them.

But it did not work out quite as she had hoped. For one thing, Alain kept chasing off after butterflies instead of talking to Lise. And for another, the widow found her neighbour such good company that after a while she actually forgot to watch her daughter. When she remembered and looked around, the little minx was talking to a handsome young man, and Alain was nowhere to be seen. I must put a stop to this, thought the widow. She called Lise to gather up the remains of the picnic and, leaving Tomas to hunt for his son, she took her daughter home.

After the hot and tiring harvest field, it felt good to be back in the cool of the kitchen. The widow settled herself in her rocking-chair and closed her eyes. Then she remembered that she should be watching her daughter, so she opened them again quickly. Lise was peering out through the window, which made her mother feel uneasy. That girl is up to something, she thought, but how can I keep a watch on her when my eyes keep falling shut? Then she had an idea.

"Get out your spinning-wheel," she told Lise, "and spin some wool. And don't think you can stop if my eyes are closed, for I shall listen for the hum of the wheel."

Lise obediently did as her mother said, but once the widow's eyes were closed, she gently edged the spinning-wheel towards the window, without breaking the rhythm of its sound. Before long, Colas appeared in the garden and the two lovers pressed their hands against the glass that separated them.

They were startled by a loud knocking at the kitchen door, which woke up the widow. Colas ducked quickly out of sight and Lise moved away from the window. She let in the harvesters who had come for their money, bringing with them a big sheaf of wheat to decorate the harvest home. The widow welcomed them, thanking them for their hard work and, when she had paid them their wages, she invited them all to the feast later in the evening.

Once they had gone, she returned to her chair. This time, the soothing hum of the wheel proved irresistible and its gentle sound was soon drowned by her loud snoring. Lise returned to the window, but Colas was nowhere to be seen. She sighed and fell to dreaming of her life when she was married to him. For once, no one was watching her, so taking the lace scarf from around her neck, she made it into a bridal veil and walked solemnly about as if she were in church. Then she took the soft bundle of wool from her spinning-wheel, wrapped it in the scarf, and rocked it in her arms as if it were her baby.

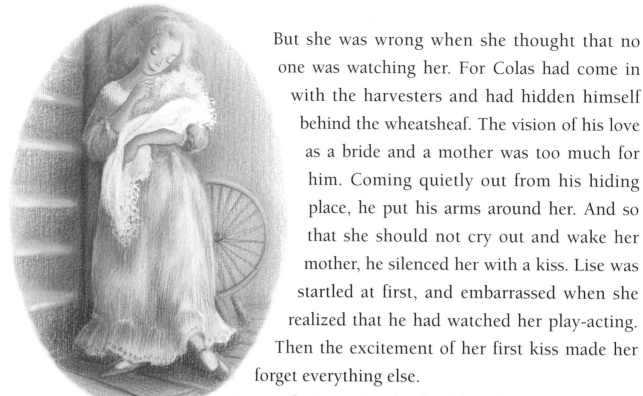

But she was wrong when she thought that no one was watching her. For Colas had come in with the harvesters and had hidden himself behind the wheatsheaf. The vision of his love as a bride and a mother was too much for him. Coming quietly out from his hiding place, he put his arms around her. And so that she should not cry out and wake her mother, he silenced her with a kiss. Lise was startled at first, and embarrassed when she realized that he had watched her play-acting. Then the excitement of her first kiss made her forget everything else.

But not for long. Another loud knock at the door made the lovers spring apart. The widow stirred in her sleep, and for a moment Lise panicked. But she thought quickly. "Upstairs," she whispered, "the only safe place is my bedroom." More loud knocking sent Colas leaping up the stairs two at a time, and covered the sound of the door slamming behind him.

"Is there no peace to be had in this house?" grumbled the widow, sleepily opening her eyes.

"Our neighbours are here," said Lise, glancing out of the window, "and another man in a dark coat."

"That will be the lawyer." The widow grew flustered. "They have brought the marriage contract. Now make yourself tidy, my girl, while I open the door."

"But, Mother," said Lise, "I have told you before: I won't marry Alain."

"Nonsense," said her mother. "You will do as you are told."

"I won't! I won't!" Lise raised her voice. "You can't make me sign it."

Another knock at the door put the poor woman in a quandary. She could not leave the visitors outside any longer, nor could she let them see her daughter behaving in this shameful and disobedient way. There was only one solution.

"Go to your room at once!" she ordered, in her most commanding voice, "and don't come down again until you are ready to sign the marriage contract."

Lise stopped short with her mouth wide open, for she was just about to refuse again. Then, to her mother's surprise, and much to her relief, she said, "Yes, Mother, I will do just as you say." And making her way meekly up the stairs, she went into the bedroom and closed the door softly behind her.

"Well," said the widow to herself, "it just shows what a firm hand will do. I knew she would come round in the end." And smoothing her dress and patting her hair into place, she went to open the door.

In came Tomas, the lawyer, with the marriage papers, and a very gloomy Alain. He stood with his head bent, his toes turned in, and a worried frown on his face.

"Well, well!" said his father. "What a joyful day this is."

"It is indeed," said the widow. "I love to see young people happy." And the two neighbours smiled warmly at one another while the papers were set out on the table.

"And where is your charming daughter?" asked the widower.

"Oh, upstairs, making herself tidy," said the widow. "A young girl likes to look her best, especially for her betrothal." She smiled coyly at Alain, who looked more miserable than ever.

"Now," said the lawyer, "I think everything is in order. If the young lady will come down, we can proceed with the signing."

"I will call her," said the widow, crossing her fingers behind her back,

and hoping for the best. "Oh, Lise," she trilled sweetly, "are you ready to come down now? Are you ready to sign your marriage contract?"

The bedroom door opened and Lise's voice, equally sweet, said, "Yes, Mother, I am coming down now. I am ready to sign." And out she came, smiling like a cat, and leading Colas by the hand.

There was a gasp of horror from the company below.

"What is this?" cried Tomas. "Has this young man been alone with your daughter? And in her bedroom? What a disgrace! Do you think that my son will marry her after this?"

"Why, no, good neighbour," said Lise, leading her lover down the stairs, "for the only contract I will sign is the one that binds me to my beloved Colas."

The poor widow was completely overcome. She gave a little moan of despair and fainted neatly into the arms of Alain, who only just caught her in time.

"Mother!" cried Lise, racing downstairs. She put her mother into the rocking-chair and fetched a damp cloth to cool her forehead. "Oh, dear Mother," she said, as the widow revived, "do try to understand. I love Colas and I could never be happy with anyone else."

"Alas!" wept the poor woman, "and it was always my dearest wish to unite our two families."

Then, to everyone's surprise, Alain spoke up for the first time. "Why, you can still do so," he said. "You have no husband and my father has no wife. Marry him, and let me have a mother again!" And, kneeling at her feet, he laid his head lovingly against her knee.

What could the widow do? She had always pitied the motherless young man: and he would probably be better off with her for a mother, than with Lise for a wife.

"My son," said Tomas, "you have spoken sense for once." He had often sampled the widow's cooking and thought it would be good to have her in his own kitchen. "I should be honoured, dear lady, if you would consent to be my wife."

This proposal put the widow into such a good humour that she wanted everyone else to be happy too.

Lise and Colas won her consent for their marriage and it was agreed that they should have her farm. She herself would move to her new husband's farm and become Alain's mother. As she thought of her new stepson, the widow sighed with pleasure. He wasn't lively, he wasn't clever, and he certainly wasn't pretty. So she would never need to watch him at all.

The Nutcracker

Clara knelt on the window seat, half hidden by the heavy curtains, and pressed her nose against the cold glass of the window. Outside, the night was still and full of mystery, with great feathery flakes of snow falling silently out of a dark sky. Behind her, the room was bright and warm and full of cheerful sounds.

Each year, on the night before Christmas, Clara's parents gave a splendid party and invited all their friends, old and young, to join in the celebrations. They were friendly people who liked nothing better than to fill their house with happy guests. But Clara, who was rather shy and awkward with strangers, found it all a little frightening. So it was that she was hiding behind the curtain, wishing that she could fly out of the window into the quiet darkness, and float magically over the rooftops with their soft white blanket of snow.

Reflected in the glass she could see the moving shapes of people dancing and, beyond them, the glow of the big Christmas tree in the far corner of the room.

"Clara! Why are you hiding there?" She sighed as her brother Franz came bouncing on to the window seat. He took hold of her hand and pulled her down into the noisy room.

"Oh, Franz!" she protested. "Can't you leave me in peace?"

"No, I can't," he said, "because Mother has sent me to find you. She has some friends who have just arrived and they want to see you."

Clara reluctantly went with him to find her mother; then she stood patiently while people patted her on the head and said how much she had grown. They all looked very much alike to her, the men in their fine clothes, the women in their silken dresses; until the last visitor arrived. He was quite different: a strange man, old and bent, he was dressed all in black and had a dark patch over one eye.

Clara's parents greeted him with affection and he did not pat her on the head or say that she had grown. Instead, he fixed his one bright eye upon her and said, very softly, "Ah . . . This one is special."

Behind the old man came servants carrying tall boxes. The guests crowded round to see what could be inside and there were cries of wonder when they were opened. Out came a tall soldier and a pretty girl, followed by a Harlequin and a Columbine. They were life-sized dolls, and when the old man wound them up with a huge key, they danced together, to the delight of the guests. The children tried to join in and, when the dancing was over, clamoured for the dolls to be wound up again. But instead, the lights were dimmed so that the Christmas tree could be seen shining in all its glory, and from beneath it Clara's parents took presents for all their friends.

As the children opened their gaily wrapped parcels, Clara felt a hand upon her shoulder and turned to see the strange old man holding out to her an oddly shaped toy. "This is a special gift," he said, "given only to one who will know its true value."

It was an ugly wooden doll with long thin legs, little short arms and a head far too big for its body. It had a funny face and a mouth full of big teeth. It was certainly not a pretty toy, but there was something so comical about it that Clara loved it at first sight. She turned to the old man with a smile that lit up her face. "Oh, thank you," she said. "I think he's lovely!"

"He is useful, too," said the old man, and reached for a nut from a piled dish nearby. Taking the doll from Clara, he showed her how to fit the nut between the big teeth and crack it by squeezing the legs together. Clara was enchanted, and so were the other children who crowded around, begging her to crack nuts for them. But Franz grew jealous; he hated to see his sister the centre of attention. Suddenly he snatched the Nutcracker from her hands and, throwing the wooden doll upon the floor, jumped on it. Clara was in tears until her father came to the rescue. He threatened to send Franz to bed if he did not behave himself, and restored the battered toy to Clara. Poor Nutcracker! His paint was scratched and his wood was dented. His comical face was more lop-sided and ugly than ever, but Clara only loved him more. She bandaged him with the white ribbon from her hair and, rocking him in her arms, she stole back to her hiding-place behind the window curtain.

The party lasted late into the night, with tired children sleeping where they fell, until their parents gathered them up to take them home.

When all the guests were gone, Franz and Clara were carried up to their nursery to be tucked into their beds. As her father lifted the sleeping Clara from her window seat, the battered Nutcracker fell from her hands and was left behind unnoticed on the floor. The lights went out, the fire died down. Time passed and the whole house grew dark and still.

Clara woke suddenly in the middle of the night: it took her a few moments to realize that she was in her bed. She sat up and felt about her for the Nutcracker, but he was nowhere to be found. She thought of him, lying alone in the great drawing-room downstairs, and she could not bear it.

Climbing out of her warm bed, she put on her slippers and tiptoed across the nursery. The moon had come out and as she went down the wide, cold staircase, she could see the world beyond the landing window shining with a snowy brightness. The white light lit up the darkened house and showed her the way. Softly, she turned the handle of the drawing-room door. As she swung it open, the draught made the dying fire flare up, filling the room with dancing shadows. Crossing the wide empty room, she heard a sudden scuttling sound and a mouse ran across the floor. Clara was rather frightened of mice, especially in the middle of the night, so she gathered up her night-dress and raced to the safety of the window seat. Leaning down, she picked up the Nutcracker and hugged him tight.

It was cosy on the window seat; she felt safe there and she did not fancy the long walk back to her room, not with mice running about the house. She pulled up the warm velvet curtain to cover herself, put her head down on the soft cushion, and closed her eyes.

It seemed only a moment later that she heard a strange scratching noise. Opening her eyes, she found the familiar drawing-room mysteriously changed. Everything seemed much larger, the spaces vast, the Christmas tree looming above her like a forest giant. It is magic, she thought a little breathlessly, and in magic anything can happen.

The scratching sound grew louder and to Clara's horror, a hoard of big, fierce mice came scurrying out of the shadows into the dancing firelight. They ran swiftly all over the room, nibbling at the gingerbread men on the Christmas tree, who had to scramble higher in an effort to escape them. Even worse, she saw a huge rat, with a crown on his head, who seemed to be their king. Poor Clara, her heart beat fast and her hands trembled for fear that he might notice her in her dark corner.

Then she heard the sound of a trumpet and out from a big box marched a troop of toy soldiers, waving their wooden swords in the air. Their leader seemed strangely familiar, with a big head and long thin legs. Clara realized with astonishment that it was her own dear Nutcracker, come to life.

She watched, holding her breath, as a fierce battle took place between the toy soldiers and the mice. Backwards and forwards they fought across the drawing-room floor, until at last the soldiers drove the mice back to their holes. Only the King Rat and the Nutcracker remained, locked in a deadly duel, and it seemed to Clara that the rat was winning. He had a fierce, sharp little sword, while the Nutcracker had only a wooden one. Suddenly the King Rat raised his sword as if he would strike to kill. Clara cried out and taking off her slipper, threw it with all her strength. It hit the King Rat in the small of his back, knocking him off balance, and at once the Nutcracker brought the wooden sword down upon his head. The big rat lay still upon the floor until the mice came out, squeaking sorrowfully, and carried him away into their mousehole.

Clara turned back to the Nutcracker and saw to her surprise that his strange big head and long thin legs were quite changed. Smiling at her and holding out her slipper was a young and handsome prince. He knelt at Clara's feet and, while he fitted the slipper on again, he thanked her for saving his life and for breaking the spell which had bound him.

"Once I lived in the kingdom of sweets," he told her, "until the terrible day when I fell under a spell and was doomed to spend my days as the ugly Nutcracker. Only when my life was saved by one who loved me in spite of my strange looks could the spell be broken."

I think I must be dreaming, thought Clara wonderingly. But if she was, she certainly did not want the dream to end.

"Now you must tell me your dearest wish," said the Nutcracker Prince, "and I shall grant it."

At first Clara could not think what to ask for, but then she remembered how she had longed to fly over the moonlit, snow-covered world beyond the window. She told the Nutcracker Prince of her dream and at once he took her by the hand. A moment later she found herself flying through a cloud of whirling snowflakes into a strange and magical world.

"I will take you to my own kingdom," said the Prince, and they swooped and soared through clouds and over snow-capped forests until, in the distance, they could see the white pinnacles of an icing-sugar castle rising up out of the snow. As they flew in through the great doorway, she saw that it had columns made of twisted barley sugar and that it was decorated with all the sweets she loved best.

Then it seemed to her that all the sweets were really alive and joyfully welcomed the Nutcracker Prince on his return.

The Prince presented Clara to the beautiful Sugar Plum Fairy who ruled as queen over the Land of Sweets. He told how she had saved his life and freed him from the magic spell. When they heard this all the sweets began to dance for joy, and Clara found that she was dancing with them. Round and round they went, faster and faster, until Clara grew quite breathless and her head was in a whirl. Then suddenly the sounds and music died, all was quiet and still, and Clara woke to the first pale light of Christmas morning.

Her first fear was that her friend the Nutcracker would be gone for ever. Anxiously she looked around but there he was on the window seat, as ugly and as comical as before. She picked him up and hugged him. "Perhaps it was magic," she told him, "or perhaps it was just a dream. But whichever it was, I shall always know that you are really a handsome prince inside."

And, clutching him in her arms, she set off back to her bedroom before the others should wake and find her missing.

The Firebird

In the great birch forests of the northern snow-line, there once lived a prince who was haunted by a dream.

He had woken one morning with the memory of a princess more radiant than sunlight upon water, and he knew that he could not rest until he found her. Lovingly, he took leave of his parents, and set out alone into the trackless wilderness.

He rode for many days, trusting his fate to guide him, for he met with no man in all the long miles he travelled. Then one evening, as the sun was sinking, he saw a flash of fire among the trees ahead of him. Dazzled, he took it for a trick of the light, until it flew up and overhead. Then he knew that he had found the Phoenix, the legendary Firebird born of flames.

The bright bird flew away and the prince followed, certain that it would lead him to the princess of his dreams. As the shadows of the trees thickened into twilight, he saw ahead of him a high stone wall barring the way. The Firebird flew up and over it and was lost from sight. Leaping from his saddle, the prince scrambled his way up the great, rough stones that reached into the dark sky. When he reached the top, he found himself gazing down into the strangest garden he had ever seen.

It was wild and overgrown and full of fearsome statues. Some were of hideous, misshapen monsters. Others, even more distressing, were of young men who seemed trapped in the stone, their limbs struggling against the stillness, their mouths crying out against the silence. Shuddering, the prince raised his eyes and saw beyond them the dark outline of a nightmare castle against the fading sky.

For a moment he longed to turn back, but then he saw the Firebird below him, eating apples from a golden tree that glowed in the dimness. It gave him the courage to climb down into the garden. Moving noiselessly through the shadows, he seized hold of the bright creature before it was aware of him. The Firebird leaped into the sky, but the prince clung to its legs. It dug fierce claws into his arms; it beat its golden wings against his face; but he would not let go. At last it grew still and, to his amazement, spoke to him in a voice like a chime of golden bells.

"Set me free!" said the Firebird, "for captivity is death to me." And indeed its strength seemed to fail in his hands.

"If I do, will you help me?" asked the prince. "I seek a princess like sunlight upon water. Do you know where she may be found?"

"She dwells in the dark castle," said the Firebird, "in the power of a cruel sorcerer whom no man can kill. Those who would rescue her, he turns to stone." The bird struggled feebly again. "Only let me go," it begged, "and I will be your friend."

"I shall have need of a friend," said the prince, and he released the shining bird.

The Firebird hovered above his head. It pulled out one of its golden tail-feathers and let it fall into the prince's hands.

"Keep it safe," said the bird, "and if you need help, wave it in the air. I will not fail you."

The next moment it was gone and the prince was alone in the darkness of the silent garden.

As he was wondering what to do next, he heard a faint, unearthly music and saw that the great doors of the castle were opening. A strange, cold light shone out from within and down the steps came twelve beautiful princesses. Their feet were bare beneath their long, white dresses and their hair hung loose about their shoulders. They moved like those who walk in their sleep, and behind them came another even more beautiful. She shone like sunlight upon water and the prince knew her from his dream.

When he stepped from the shadows, the princess started and grew pale.

"Do not be afraid," he said gently. "I have come to save you from this awful place."

"It is for you that I fear," said the princess. "The Sorcerer's magic is too powerful. If he finds you here, he will turn you to stone. Leave this place as swiftly as you can and think of me no more."

The prince took her hand. "You filled my thoughts when you were only a dream," he told her; "do you think I can forget you now that I have seen your face? It is my fate to love you and yours to be my bride."

"Alas!" said the princess, "there is no escape for us. For a little while each night we walk in the garden, but we cannot pass beyond the wall and, when day breaks, we must return into our dark prison. While the Sorcerer lives, we can never be free."

"Then he must die!" said the prince, and he drew his sword.

But the princess told him that the Sorcerer's soul was hidden inside an egg which was locked in an iron box and buried in a secret place. "Swords cannot touch him," she said. "Only if the egg is broken, can he be destroyed."

When the first light of dawn crept into the sky, the princesses turned and moved slowly back up the steps into the castle. As the great doors began to close, the prince tried to follow, but the very air made a barrier through which he could not pass.

In his despair, the prince cried out and struck at the stone steps with his sword. At once, the garden was filled with hideous sounds; the monstrous statues began to move and then to walk. They crowded around the prince, seizing hold of him with bony hands and fierce claws and clinging tentacles.

There was a loud clap of thunder and a vivid flash of lightning. The doors creaked open and down the steps came the tall figure of the Sorcerer, his eyes cold with anger in his shadowed face.

He laughed when he saw the prince, but it was a cruel and mocking laugh. "Have you come for my princess?" he demanded. "Did you think to steal away the fairest, the one above all others I have chosen for my bride?"

The prince tried to rush at him, but already his feet seemed to have lost the power of movement. As if in some terrible nightmare, he found that he was turning to stone, his struggles freezing into grotesque contortions.

Then he remembered the Firebird. With the one hand that he could still move, he pulled the feather from inside his jacket, and waved it above his head. In a moment the great bird was there, its golden plumage lighting up the dark garden.

The magic of the Firebird was even more powerful than that of the Sorcerer. Soaring and swooping, it cast a spell over him and all the monsters, so that they fell into a deep and heavy sleep, while the prince found himself able to move again.

"Quickly!" said the Firebird, "the spell will not last for long. Dig where I will show you. You must find the box which holds the egg in which the Sorcerer's soul lies buried."

The prince dug with his sword and, when that broke, he dug on with his bare hands, in spite of the sharp stones that cut and bruised him. As his fingers felt the smooth lid of the box, he saw that the monsters were beginning to move and that one of the Sorcerer's evil eyes was open. Tearing the box from its hiding place, he struggled to open it, but it was securely locked.

The monsters were on their feet, circling around him: the Sorcerer raised his thin arms, with his magic staff in his hands. Lightning flashed and thunder rolled across the sky.

The Firebird flew over him and dropped a golden feather: it drifted down onto the box and the lid sprang open. The prince seized the egg but already the monsters were upon him. He raised it and with his last strength, threw it high above their heads.

Every hand, every claw, every grasping tentacle reached up to save it, but it was too late. The egg fell to earth, struck against a rock and shattered into a thousand fragments. There was one last, terrible cry and then silence. The Sorcerer and his monsters vanished as if they had never been.

As the light grew, the garden was transformed: birds began to sing and buds to open; the statues of the writhing men moved and changed. The castle doors opened and the twelve princesses ran out, laughing and joyful, each to be claimed by her own loving prince.

Behind them, shimmering like sunlight upon water, came the loveliest princess of all. As the prince gathered her into his arms, the Firebird soared above them, glowing like the red-gold sun which now rose above the rim of the world, bringing in the new day.

Notes on the Ballets

The Song of the Nightingale

Music by Stravinsky; choreography by Leonide Massine.

First presented in Paris in 1920 by Diaghilev's Ballets Russes, the ballet was revived by that company in 1925, with choreography by George Balanchine. Alicia Markova, at fourteen the youngest dancer ever to belong to the Ballets Russes, danced the title role. It was first performed in America in 1926.

The Song of the Nightingale is based on Hans Christian Andersen's story *The Nightingale*, and was originally composed as an opera.

Giselle

Music by Adam; choreography by Jules Perrot and Jean Coralli.

Immediately acclaimed as the greatest ballet of all time, *Giselle* remains perhaps the most important ballet of the Romantic era, although many changes have occurred over the years and we do not know precisely how much of the present choreography is original. It was first performed in Paris in 1841, London in 1842, and in Boston in 1846.

Giselle was inspired by the story (popular in the literature of the time) of the Wilis, the spirits of maidens who entice men to their deaths.

Coppelia

Music by Delibes; choreography by Arthur Saint-Léon.

The most famous comedy ballet of all time, but with a tragic story attached to the first dancer to take the principal role. Guiseppina Bozacchi died of smallpox on the morning of her seventeenth birthday, only six months after creating the role of Coppelia. The ballet was first performed in Paris in 1870, in New York in 1887, and in London in 1906.

Coppelia is based on a Gothic tale, *Dr Coppelius*, by the German storyteller, Hoffmann.

Swan Lake

Music by Tchaikovsky; choreography by Marius Petipa and Lev Ivanov.

Swan Lake is perhaps the most popular classical ballet, and is always changing. There are numerous versions and most companies around the world include at least a one act version in their repertory. The first production, in 1877, was incomplete and unsuccessful. It was presented in its complete form to great acclaim in Russia in 1895, in New York in 1911, and in London in 1934.

Petrushka

Music by Stravinsky; choreography by Michel Fokine.

First performed by Diaghilev's Ballets Russes in Paris in 1911 with Vaslav Nijinsky as Petrushka, the ballet was presented in New York in 1916, and was revived by the Royal Ballet in London in 1957.

Stravinsky wrote *Petrushka* originally as a piece for piano and orchestra.

The Boy and the Magic (*L'Enfant et les Sortilèges*)

Music by Ravel; choreography by George Balanchine.

The ballet was first presented in Monte Carlo in 1935, and in New York in 1946.

L'Enfant et les Sortilèges is based on a poem by Colette. The music, wrote Ravel, "was composed in the spirit of an American musical comedy".

The Girl Who Needed Watching (*La Fille Mal Gardée*)

Music by Hérold; choreography by Jean Dauberval.

The oldest ballet in the current repertory, *La Fille Mal Gardée* is regarded as a turning point in the history of ballet. For the first time, ballet was used to tell a story, rather than being only a series of formal dances. It was first performed in Bordeaux and Paris in 1789, in London in 1791, and in New York in 1794. Today's most often performed version was choreographed by Sir Frederick Ashton for the Royal Ballet in 1960.

The Nutcracker

Music by Tchaikovsky; choreography by Lev Ivanov.

The ballet was first performed in St Petersburg in 1892, and in London in 1934. In America it was first presented in a shortened form in New York in 1940, with a full-length performance by the San Francisco Ballet in 1944. There are now a number of different versions of this Christmas favourite regularly danced.

The Nutcracker is based on a tale by Hoffmann.

The Firebird

Music by Stravinsky; choreography by Michel Fokine.

First presented by Diaghilev's Ballets Russes in Paris in 1910, it was first performed in New York in 1955, and in Edinburgh and London in 1954. A version choreographed by George Balanchine was first performed in New York in 1949.

The Firebird is based on a Russian legend.